I0477898

UNLOCKING THE KEY TO FINANCIAL
FREEDOM: budgeting,save more,get out of
debt,live a calm life and lasting monetary
freedom.

Scott N.Tripp

All rights reserved. No part of this publication may be reproduced,distributed,or transmitted in any form or by any means, including photocopying, recording or other electronic or mechanical methods, without the prior written permission of the publisher, except in the case of brief quotations embodied in critical reviews and certain other non-commercial uses permitted by copyright law.

Copyright © Scott N Tripp

Introduction

Opening the way to independence from the rat race is something other than a slippery dream — it's an unmistakable reality that innumerable people can achieve through careful monetary administration. Envision a day to day existence where you're not generally troubled by the stifling load of obligation, where your reserve funds consistently develop, and your spending plan works flawlessly, enabling you instead of compelling you. This vision of independence from the rat race isn't only for the fortunate few; it's inside your range assuming that you saddle the right techniques and outlook.

At its center, independence from the rat race implies having an adequate number of reserve funds, ventures, and money available to manage the cost of the way of life you need for you as well as your loved ones. It's tied in with developing those reserve funds and speculations to produce a pay that gives the opportunity to seek after interests, venture to the far corners of the planet, or essentially appreciate existence without monetary pressure. Accomplishing this degree of monetary freedom includes a few basic advances: planning shrewdly, saving more, taking out obligation, and developing a mentality equipped towards long haul monetary wellbeing.

The excursion to independence from the rat race starts with a very much organized spending plan. Planning isn't tied in with confining your spending to the mark of uneasiness; rather, about pursuing informed choices line up with your monetary objectives. Begin by following your pay and costs carefully. Comprehend where your cash is going every month, and distinguish regions where you can scale back without forfeiting your personal satisfaction. The 50/30/20 rule can be a useful rule: designate half of your pay to needs, 30% to needs, and 20% to reserve funds and obligation reimbursement. By sticking to a spending plan, you make a reasonable guide for your funds, guaranteeing you live inside your means and stay away from pointless obligation.

Independence from the rat race isn't just about numbers; it's about inner serenity. At the point when you're not continually stressed over cash, you can zero in more on getting a charge out of life and seeking after your interests. Monetary pressure can adversely affect mental and actual wellbeing, prompting nervousness, discouragement, and other medical problems. By accomplishing monetary soundness, you lessen pressure and further develop your general prosperity. It permits you to go with choices in view of what's best for yourself as well as your family, as opposed to what you can bear right now.

Chapter 1

Understanding the basics of budgeting
* What is budget
A budget is a monetary arrangement that frameworks anticipated pay and costs over a predetermined period, normally a month or a year. It fills in as a guide for dealing with your funds, assisting you with dispensing assets effectively to meet your monetary objectives, control spending, and save for future requirements.

Key Parts of a Spending plan

Pay/Wages: Standard pay from business.

Rewards/Commissions: Extra profit from work execution.

Premium/Profits: Pay from ventures.

Different Sources: Rental pay, independent work, and so on.

Elements of a spending plan

Arranging and Allotment:

Designates pay towards fundamental costs, optional spending, and reserve funds objectives.

Guarantees that spending lines up with monetary needs and objectives.

Following and Control:

Screens genuine spending against arranged costs.

Distinguishes regions where overspending may happen, taking into consideration change

Objective Setting:

Works with defining Obligation is a strong monetary instrument that, when utilized dependably, can assist with accomplishing critical objectives and work on monetary prosperity. In any case, it likewise requires cautious administration to keep away from the traps of exorbitant interest costs, monetary pressure, and credit harm.

By figuring out the sorts of obligation, the explanations behind getting, and compelling obligation the executives procedures, people and organizations can use obligation for their potential benefit while keeping up with monetary solidness.

Monetary Discipline:

Empowers mindful spending and saving propensities.

Forestalls drive buys and stays away from pointless obligation.

Monetary Security:

Constructs a wellbeing net by guaranteeing normal commitments to reserve funds and crisis reserves.

Gets ready for surprising costs and future monetary requirements.

Making a spending plan

Survey Pay:

Work out all kinds of revenue, both standard and sporadic.

List Costs:

Archive every single month to month cost, including fixed, variable, and optional expenses.

Think about yearly costs and designate a month to month segment for them.

Put forth Objectives:

Characterize present moment and long haul monetary objectives.

Decide how much cash should be dispensed towards these objectives every month.

Plan and Change:
Contrast complete pay with all out costs.
Change spending to guarantee that costs don't surpass pay.

Obligation is a strong monetary instrument that, when utilized dependably, can assist with accomplishing critical objectives and work on monetary prosperity. In any case, it likewise requires cautious administration to keep away from the traps of exorbitant interest costs, monetary pressure, and credit harm.

By figuring out the sorts of obligation, the explanations behind getting, and compelling obligation the executives procedures, people and organizations can use obligation for their potential benefit while keeping up with monetary solidness. Use planning apparatuses or applications to follow spending and make changes depending on the situation.
By keeping a spending plan, people and families can oversee their funds, pursue informed monetary choices, and work towards accomplishing long haul monetary strength and freedom.

Chapter 2

The Importance of Saving

Setting aside cash is a basic part of monetary wellbeing and soundness. It gives a pad against unforeseen costs, considers future ventures, and gives you the opportunity to seek after your objectives and dreams without monetary pressure. Reserve funds empower you to make arrangements for significant life altering situations, like purchasing a home, financing schooling, or resigning serenely. Besides, having a hearty reserve funds propensity constructs monetary discipline and diminishes dependence using a loan, encouraging long haul monetary freedom and security.

Motivations to Set aside Cash

Backup stash:
Life is flighty, and unforeseen costs can emerge whenever, for example, health related crises, vehicle fixes, or employment misfortune. A secret stash goes about as a monetary wellbeing net, keeping you from turning to exorbitant interest obligation during troublesome times

Significant Buys:
Saving permits you to manage the cost of massive costs, like purchasing a home, a vehicle, or financing a wedding, without depending on credits. It additionally furnishes influence to make enormous buys with better monetary terms.

Retirement:
Building a retirement store guarantees that you can keep up with your way of life and cover costs when you're done working. The previous you begin putting something aside for retirement, the more you can profit from build interest.

Instruction:
Putting something aside for instruction, whether for yourself or your kids, can assist with covering educational expenses, books, and other related costs. This interest in schooling can open up better vocation open doors and higher acquiring potential.

Monetary Objectives:

Whether it's beginning a business, voyaging, or seeking after a side interest, having reserve funds empowers you to accomplish individual and monetary objectives without disturbing your spending plan.

Peace of mind:

Knowing you have savings set aside provides a sense of security and reduces financial stress. This peace of mind allows you to focus on other aspects of life without constantly worrying about money.

Tips to Empower Investment funds

Make a Financial plan:

Begin by following your pay and costs to comprehend where your cash is going. A financial plan assists you with distinguishing regions where you can scale back and designate more towards reserve funds

Put forth Reserve funds Objectives:

Characterize clear, feasible investment funds objectives, whether present moment (like putting something aside for an excursion) or long haul (like purchasing a house). Having explicit objectives gives you an objective to pursue and keeps you propelled.

Mechanize Investment funds:

Set up programmed moves from your financial records to your bank account. This guarantees that a part of your pay is saved before you get an opportunity to spend it.

Cut Pointless Costs:

Audit your ways of managing money and distinguish trivial costs that you can diminish or take out. Little changes, such as feasting out less or dropping unused memberships, can accumulate over the long haul.

Pay Yourself First:

Treat reserve funds as really important by distributing a piece of your pay to investment funds prior to covering different bills. This approach guarantees that you reliably set aside cash every month.

Use Investment funds Applications:
Use monetary applications and instruments that assist you with following spending, oversee financial plans, and put forth investment funds objectives. These applications can likewise give experiences into your monetary propensities and propose regions for development.

Increment Pay:
Search for potential chances to support your pay, like agreeing with on a particular stance work, outsourcing, or selling unused things. Extra pay can be guided towards reserve funds to arrive at your objectives quicker.

Exploit Boss Projects:
In the event that your boss offers retirement plans, for example, a 401(k), or matching commitments, make the most of these projects. They can fundamentally improve your reserve funds over the long run.

Remain Restrained:
Adhere to your financial plan and investment funds plan, in any event, while spending on superfluous items is enticing. Consistently audit your headway and make changes depending on the situation to keep focused.

Stay away from Obligation:
Limit the utilization of Mastercards and try not to assume exorbitant interest obligation. Center around taking care of existing obligations to let loose more cash for investment funds.

By integrating these tips into your monetary everyday practice, you can fabricate areas of strength for a for setting aside cash. Reliable saving gives monetary security as well as engages you to accomplish your fantasies and partake in a tranquil monetary future.

Chapter 3

Investing

Understanding Investing

Investing is the act of allocating resources, usually money, with the expectation of generating an income or profit. It's a crucial aspect of building wealth and achieving financial goals. By investing, you can make your money work for you, potentially growing your initial sum over time through appreciation, dividends, or interest. While it involves risk, the potential rewards make investing an essential strategy for long-term financial planning.

Importance of Investing

Wealth Accumulation:
Investing allows your money to grow over time through compound interest and market appreciation. Unlike saving, which typically offers lower returns, investing has the potential to significantly increase your wealth.

Inflation Hedge:
Inflation reduces the purchasing power of money over time. Investments, particularly in assets like stocks and real estate, typically outpace inflation, helping to preserve and increase your wealth.

Income Generation:
Certain investments, such as bonds, dividend-paying stocks, and rental properties, provide regular income. This can supplement your primary income and offer financial stability.

Achieving Financial Goals:
Investing can help you reach significant financial milestones, such as buying a home, funding education, or starting a business. It enables you to grow your capital and achieve these goals more quickly than relying solely on savings.

Types of Investment

Stocks:
Address proprietorship in an organization. Stocks offer high development potential yet accompanied higher gamble. Financial backers acquire returns through value appreciation and profits.

Bonds:
Obligation protections gave by states or enterprises. Bonds give ordinary interest installments and are for the most part safer than stocks, making them a steady pay source

Shared Assets and ETFs:
Pooled speculation vehicles that permit financial backers to expand across a scope of resources. They are overseen by experts and proposition expansion, decreasing gamble.

Land:
Includes buying property to procure rental pay or for cost appreciation. Land can give stable returns and go about as an unmistakable resource.

Products:
Actual merchandise like gold, oil, or rural items. Items can enhance a portfolio and fence against expansion yet can be unstable.

Cryptographic forms of money:
Computerized or virtual monetary standards that utilization cryptography for security. Cryptographic forms of money like Bitcoin offer high possible returns yet are exceptionally unstable and speculative.

Tips for Fruitful Money Management

Begin Early:
The previous you start financial planning, the additional time your cash needs to develop. Accumulate revenue amplifies returns over the long run, making early money management especially advantageous.

Expand:
Spread your speculations across various resource classes and areas to decrease risk. Broadening mitigates the effect of a poor-performing venture on your general portfolio.

Grasp Your Gamble Resilience:
Survey how much gamble you're happy with taking. More youthful financial backers could face more gamble challenges better yields, while those nearer to retirement might favor more secure speculations.

No about investment options, market trends, and financial strategies. Continuous learning helps you make informed decisions and adapt to changing market conditions.

Set Clear Goals:
Define your financial objectives and investment timeline. Having clear goals guides your investment strategy and helps you stay focused.

Invest Regularly:
Consistent investing, such as dollar-cost averaging, reduces the impact of market volatility. Regular contributions build wealth steadily over time.

Avoid Emotional Decisions:
Markets can be volatile, and emotions can lead to impulsive decisions. Stick to your investment plan and avoid reacting to short-term market fluctuations.

Review and Adjust:
Periodically review your investment portfolio to ensure it aligns with your goals and risk tolerance. Make adjustments as needed based on performance and changes in your financial situation.

Seek Professional Advice:
Consider consulting with a financial advisor, especially if you're new to investing. A professional can provide personalized guidance and help you develop.

Be Patient:
Investing is a long-term endeavor. Stay patient and give your investments time to grow. Avoid the temptation to chase quick profits, as this can lead to significant losses.

Investing is an integral asset for creating financial momentum, accomplishing monetary objectives, and getting your future. By figuring out the significance of effective money management, expanding your portfolio, and pursuing informed choices, you can tackle the capability of the monetary business sectors to develop your cash. Whether you're putting something aside for retirement, subsidizing training, or looking for monetary freedom, contributing can assist you with arriving at your goals and give a stable monetary establishment to years to come.

Investment Strategy: Building Wealth for the Future
An effective investment strategy is essential for growing your wealth and achieving long-term financial goals. Whether you're saving for retirement, a major purchase, or simply to build financial security, a well-planned investment strategy can help you make informed decisions and maximize your returns. Here's an overview of key components and approaches to crafting a successful investment strategy.

Spread Your Investments:

Diversification involves spreading investments across various asset classes (stocks, bonds, real estate, etc.) to reduce risk. This strategy can protect your portfolio from significant losses.

Include Different Sectors and Geographies:

Within each asset class, diversify across different sectors and geographical regions to further minimize risk.

Determine the Right Mix:

Asset allocation is the process of deciding how to distribute your investments among different asset classes. The right mix depends on your risk tolerance, time horizon, and financial goals.

Periodically review and adjust your asset allocation to stay aligned with your changing financial situation and market conditions.

Investment Strategies
Growth Investing:

Focuses on investing in companies expected to grow at an above-average rate. This strategy seeks capital appreciation but may involve higher risk.

Value Investing:

Involves picking undervalued stocks that are trading below their intrinsic value. This approach looks for bargains in the market.

Income Investing:

Prioritizes investments that generate regular income, such as dividends from stocks or interest from bonds. Suitable for investors seeking steady cash flow.

Dollar-Cost Averaging:

Invest a fixed amount of money at regular intervals, regardless of market conditions. This strategy reduces the impact of market volatility and can lower the average cost of investments over time.

Chapter 4

Debt

Debt is a financial obligation that arises when an individual, business, or government borrows money from a lender with the agreement to repay the borrowed amount, often with interest, over a specified period. It is a common financial tool used for various purposes, such as purchasing a home, funding education, or expanding a business. While debt can provide opportunities to achieve significant goals, it also carries risks and responsibilities that require careful management.

At its center, obligation can be ordered into two fundamental sorts: got and unstable. Gotten obligation, for example, home loans and car advances, is upheld by insurance, meaning the moneylender has the privilege to hold onto the resource assuming the borrower defaults. Uncollateralized debt, similar to Visas and individual credits, doesn't need security yet frequently accompanies higher loan fees to make up for the expanded gamble to the moneylender.

Overseeing obligation successfully requires an essential methodology. It's fundamental to comprehend the provisions of any obligation you take on, including loan costs, reimbursement plans, and any related expenses. Making a spending plan that records for obligation installments and focusing on exorbitant interest obligation can assist with forestalling monetary strain.

While obligation can give fundamental monetary influence, unreasonable or inadequately oversaw obligation can prompt huge monetary pressure and long haul outcomes. Understanding how to utilize obligation shrewdly, perceiving the admonition indications of obligation over-burden, and knowing the systems for obligation decrease are principal to keeping up with monetary strength and accomplishing long haul monetary objectives. Whether you're hoping to oversee existing obligation or pondering assuming new obligation, informed choices and restrained monetary propensities are fundamental for utilizing obligation as a positive device in your monetary tool compartment.

Types of Debt

1 Personal Debt:
Credit Card Debt: This is one of the most common forms of debt, where individuals use credit cards for everyday purchases. Credit card debt often carries high interest rates, making it expensive if not paid off monthly.

Personal Loans: These are unsecured loans taken out for various purposes, such as consolidating debt, home improvements, or medical expenses. Personal loans typically have fixed interest rates and repayment terms.

Auto Loans: Loans used to purchase vehicles. These loans are secured by the vehicle itself and typically have lower interest rates than unsecured loans.

2 Mortgages:
Loans used to buy real estate, typically with the property itself serving as collateral. Mortgages usually have lower interest rates and long repayment periods, such as 15 or 30 years.

3 Business Debt:
Business Loans: Borrowed funds used to start, run, or expand a business. These loans can be secured or unsecured and may come with various terms based on the business's creditworthiness and the purpose of the loan.

Lines of Credit: Flexible loan arrangements that provide businesses with access to a fixed amount of capital, which they can draw upon as needed.

4 Government Debt:

Treasury Bonds: Debt securities issued by the government to finance various public projects and operations. These bonds are considered low-risk and pay periodic interest to investors.

Municipal Bonds: Issued by local governments or municipalities to fund public projects like schools, highways, and infrastructure improvements.

Managing Debt Effectively

1 Create a Budget:
Develop a budget to track income and expenses, ensuring that you allocate sufficient funds to repay your debts. A budget helps identify areas where you can cut back on spending and allocate more towards debt repayment.

2 Prioritize High-Interest Debt:
Focus on paying off high-interest debt first, such as credit card balances, to reduce the overall interest you pay and accelerate debt repayment.

3 Make Consistent Payments:
Always make at least the minimum payments on your debts to avoid penalties and damage to your credit score. Aim to pay more than the minimum whenever possible to reduce the principal faster.

4 Consider Debt Consolidation:
Consolidate multiple debts into a single loan with a lower interest rate to simplify repayment and potentially save on interest costs.

5 Negotiate with Creditors:
If you're struggling to make payments, contact your creditors to negotiate better terms, such as lower interest rates or extended repayment periods.

6 Seek Professional Help:
If your debt situation is overwhelming, consider consulting with a financial advisor or a credit counseling service to develop a debt management plan.

Chapter 5

Staying on track: Strategies for success

Here are some strategies to help you stay on track and achieve your desired outcomes:

- Set Clear Goal:

1 Define Your Objectives:
Clearly articulate what you want to achieve. Whether it's completing a project, reaching a fitness milestone, or advancing in your career, having a clear goal provides direction and motivation.

2 Make Goals SMART:
Ensure your goals are Specific, Measurable, Achievable, Relevant, and Time-bound. This framework helps clarify your objectives and increases the likelihood of success.

- Develop a Plan
1 Break Down Goals into Tasks:
Divide larger goals into smaller, actionable tasks. This makes them more manageable and allows you to track progress more effectively.

2 Create a Timeline:
Set deadlines for each task to create a sense of urgency and accountability. Having a timeline helps you stay focused and ensures steady progress towards your goals.

- Stay Organized
1 Use a Planner or Calendar:
Keep track of deadlines, appointments, and tasks using a planner or digital calendar. Schedule regular check-ins to review your progress and adjust your plan as needed.

2 Prioritize Tasks:

Identify the most important tasks and tackle them first. This helps you focus on high-impact activities and prevents procrastination.

- Manage Time Effectively

1 Minimize Distractions:
Identify common distractions and take steps to minimize them. This may involve setting boundaries with technology, creating a dedicated workspace, or using time-blocking techniques.

2 Practice Time Management Techniques:
Use strategies like the Pomodoro Technique or time blocking to structure your day and maximize productivity. Break tasks into focused work intervals followed by short breaks to maintain concentration.

- Stay Motivated

1 Find Your Why:
Connect your goals to your deeper values and motivations. Understanding why you want to achieve something can provide the inspiration and drive needed to stay on track, especially during challenging times.

2 Celebrate Progress:
Acknowledge and celebrate your achievements along the way. Whether it's completing a task, reaching a milestone, or overcoming a hurdle, celebrating small wins boosts morale and reinforces positive behaviors.

- Stay Accountable

1 Share Your Goals:
Share your goals with a trusted friend, mentor, or accountability partner. Knowing that someone else is aware of your objectives can increase your commitment and provide encouragement.

2 Track Your Progress:

Keep track of your progress using visual aids, such as progress charts or habit trackers. Seeing how far you've come can motivate you to continue moving forward.

- Adapt and Adjust

1 Be Flexible:

Be open to adapting your plan based on changing circumstances or new information. Flexibility allows you to respond to challenges and setbacks without losing sight of your ultimate objectives.

2 Learn from Setbacks:

View setbacks as learning opportunities rather than failures. Reflect on what went wrong, adjust your approach if necessary, and use the experience to improve future performance.

- Cultivate Resilience

1 Practice Self-Care:

Prioritize self-care activities that promote physical, mental, and emotional well-being. Taking care of yourself ensures you have the energy and resilience needed to stay on track.

2 Develop a Growth Mindset:

Embrace challenges as opportunities for growth and learning. Cultivate a mindset that views setbacks as temporary obstacles rather than insurmountable barriers.

- Stay Consistent

1 Establish Habits:

Develop routines and habits that support your goals. Consistent actions over time lead to meaningful progress and lasting results.

2 Stay Committed:

Stay committed to your goals, even when progress is slow or obstacles arise. Remember why you started and keep pushing forward with determination and resilience.

Staying on track is crucial for achieving your long-term goals, whether they pertain to personal growth, career advancement, financial success, or overall well-being. The journey towards your objectives is often fraught with distractions, setbacks, and challenges, but maintaining focus and commitment is the key to overcoming these obstacles.

Setting clear, realistic goals is the foundation of staying on track. When your objectives are well-defined, it becomes easier to create actionable plans and prioritize tasks that align with your desired outcomes. Developing a detailed roadmap, complete with milestones and deadlines, helps in tracking progress and making necessary adjustments along the way.

Time management and organization are vital components of staying on track. Utilizing tools such as planners, calendars, and productivity apps can help you allocate your time efficiently and keep your daily activities aligned with your goals. Additionally, minimizing distractions and creating a conducive environment for focused work enhances your ability to stay committed to your plans.

Equally important is the need to stay motivated and resilient. Celebrating small victories along the way and reflecting on your progress can boost morale and reinforce your dedication. Accountability, whether through self-monitoring or involving others, provides an extra layer of commitment and support.

Staying on track requires intention, discipline, and perseverance. By setting clear goals, developing a plan, staying organized, managing time effectively, staying motivated, and cultivating resilience, you can overcome obstacles and achieve your objectives. Remember to stay flexible, adapt to changing circumstances, and celebrate your progress along the way. With dedication and effort, you can stay on track and make meaningful strides towards your desired outcomes.

Conclusion

In the mission for independence from the rat race, excelling at planning, saving tirelessly, breaking liberated from obligation, and embracing a tranquil way of life are the keys that open the way to enduring success. As you explore the exciting bends in the road of your monetary excursion, recall that each dollar saved, each obligation paid off, and each planned cost carries you nearer to the final location: monetary freedom.

Planning fills in as your guide, directing your monetary choices and guaranteeing that your assets are dispensed carefully. Saving more than you spend not just forms a wellbeing net for what's in store yet in addition enables you to seek after your fantasies without the weight of monetary pressure. Escaping obligation frees you from the shackles of revenue installments, permitting you to divert your well deserved cash towards creating financial stability.

Embracing a tranquil way of life goes past monetary contemplations; it's tied in with discovering a sense of harmony of psyche and happiness in each part of life. By focusing on monetary prosperity and rehearsing careful spending, you establish the groundwork for a future where monetary concerns never again direct your bliss.

In this way, jump all over the chance to assume command over your funds today. With devotion, discipline, and a promise to your monetary objectives, you can open the way to independence from the rat race and leave on an excursion towards a more splendid, more prosperous future.

www.ingramcontent.com/pod-product-compliance
Lightning Source LLC
Chambersburg PA
CBHW030047230526
45472CB00005B/1709